Fried Chips

John Shenton

Published by John Shenton, 2024.

FRIED CHIPS

First edition. September 25, 2024.

ISBN: 979-8224387106

Written by John Shenton.

Also by John Shenton

Business Plan Basics
The Bahamas - More Islands and Recipes Than You Expect!
Collected Musings from Bricks and Mortar to E-commerce
The Smart City Odyssey: Unveiling the Secrets to Traveller-Centric
Software
The Dragon's Gambit: China's Bid for Global Dominance and the
Western Response
Silent Weapon
Business Basics: Money Sources
Influx
Fried Chips
Mandates, Motors, and Misinformation
Echos of Orwell
Control and Chaos
The Empire's Warning: What Rome's Fall Tells Us About the West
Today

Table of Contents

Foreword

In the modern era, the battlefield has evolved beyond the physical realm into a domain defined by data, circuits, and the unseen power of digital warfare. The following chapters explore a future in which the tools of destruction are no longer merely tanks, missiles, or infantry but algorithms, microchips, and covert sabotage. This book provides a thorough and sobering analysis of the challenges we face as we enter an age where wars are fought with lines of code, and the most valuable asset a nation holds is its technology.

At the heart of this work is the concept of hybrid warfare: a fusion of conventional military force, irregular tactics, and increasingly, cyber operations. The reliance on technology for nearly every facet of modern life national defence, energy grids, transportation networks, and even individual devices has created new vulnerabilities that hostile actors can exploit with devastating precision. The consequences of these vulnerabilities are stark and far-reaching: cyber espionage, sabotage, infrastructure collapse, and the potential for broader military conflict loom large in the chapters ahead.

Through a detailed exploration of known actors China, Russia, Iran, and North Korea the reader is introduced to the geopolitical landscape of cyber warfare. These nations, equipped with sophisticated capabilities, are reshaping the global balance of power. The theft of intellectual property, tampering with hardware at the production stage, and deliberate introduction of malware into critical systems are just some of the methods examined in this book. Perhaps most alarming is the potential for chip-level sabotage and electromagnetic pulse (EMP) strikes that could cripple entire societies. What emerges is a world where civilians, not just soldiers, are at the front lines of a digital arms race.

The stakes of failing to address these threats are dire. Left unmitigated, the next war may not be fought on land, sea, or in the air but in the very systems that sustain modern civilization. A targeted EMP strike or widespread digital sabotage could lead to economic collapse, societal disintegration, and even famine. Power grids could be knocked offline for months, emergency services rendered useless, and critical infrastructure crippled. The long-term effects of such a catastrophe would be felt for generations.

However, as the book stresses, the future of warfare in the digital domain is not predetermined. It can be shaped by the actions of strong leadership in the United States, Canada, the United Kingdom, and Western Europe. Yet the current climate of appeasement by political leaders who favour globalism and passive diplomacy over decisive action threatens the security of the West. Without firm resolve and a renewed commitment to technological innovation and defence, we risk ceding ground to those who would use these new forms of warfare to achieve their strategic aims.

At its core, this book is both a call to arms and a roadmap for resilience. It urges not only the strengthening of national defence strategies but also the fostering of international cooperation. This cooperation is essential, not just for deterrence but for developing the technological means to protect critical infrastructure and national security. The private sector, too, plays a pivotal role, as corporations are increasingly responsible for securing the technology upon which all modern economies depend.

In reading the following chapters, the reader will come to understand that the future of warfare is already upon us. The war for control of digital systems and the technology that underpins them is being fought daily by spies, hackers, and saboteurs working in the shadows. The question we must ask ourselves is whether we are prepared to meet this threat or if we will allow complacency to lead us to failure.

The consequences of inaction are stark, and this book provides both a warning and a strategy to ensure that the free world remains secure in the face of this evolving threat. We stand at a critical juncture; the choices we make today will determine whether our societies can withstand the coming storm or whether they will falter in the face of a new kind of warfare. The stakes could not be higher, and the time for action is now.

Chapter 1: Introduction to Hybrid Warfare in the Digital Age

Overview: Defining Hybrid Warfare in the 21st Century

Hybrid warfare is a strategic approach that blends conventional military operations with irregular tactics and advanced cyber capabilities, creating a multifaceted battlefield that spans physical, digital, and psychological domains. Unlike traditional warfare, which relies primarily on direct military engagement, hybrid warfare capitalises on a broad spectrum of tools, including cyberattacks, disinformation, and economic coercion. These tactics undermine an opponent's ability to defend itself, both militarily and socially.

The concept of hybrid warfare is not entirely new. Throughout history, militaries have employed non-conventional tactics to subvert their enemies, from guerrilla warfare to espionage. However, with the rise of modern technology, especially the internet and advanced computing, hybrid warfare has transformed into a far more sophisticated and dangerous form of conflict. The digital age has created an environment where cyberattacks and electronic warfare can be launched remotely, targeting critical infrastructure without direct military confrontation.

Hybrid warfare thrives in the blurred lines between peace and conflict. By leveraging digital tools, state and non-state actors can achieve strategic objectives without triggering full-scale war. This ambiguity complicates the response from the targeted state, which must navigate a mixture of physical attacks, cyber intrusions, and psychological operations in a landscape where the boundaries between civilian and military spheres are increasingly intertwined.

Key Themes in Hybrid Warfare

1. Digital Vulnerabilities

The rapid digitization of national infrastructure and services has created new vulnerabilities that adversaries in hybrid warfare can exploit. Governments, financial systems, energy grids, and military operations have become highly dependent on interconnected digital systems. While these systems have increased efficiency and integration, they have also exposed nations to unprecedented risks. A well-placed cyberattack can cripple power grids, disrupt financial markets, or disable communication systems, causing widespread societal disruption without the need for a single shot to be fired.

The most significant challenge in defending against hybrid warfare lies in the invisible nature of many attacks. Unlike physical assaults, where the damage is immediate and observable, cyberattacks can occur in the shadows, often without immediate detection. Adversaries can infiltrate networks, extract sensitive information, and lay the groundwork for future sabotage long before their presence is discovered.

The challenge of defending against digital vulnerabilities is compounded by the fact that most national infrastructures power grids, water supplies, and transportation systems are operated by private entities. This diffusion of responsibility across public and private sectors means that coordination in defending against cyber threats can be slow and inefficient. Adversaries can exploit these gaps in communication and protection, making hybrid warfare a preferred tool for disrupting an enemy's society at its core.

2. Evolution of Integrated Circuits

The development of modern hybrid warfare is intricately linked to the evolution of integrated circuits (ICs) and microchips. These components form the backbone of nearly all modern electronic devices, from smartphones to military hardware. The miniaturization of ICs has allowed for the rapid proliferation of advanced technology, but it has also increased the number of vulnerabilities available to adversaries in the digital space.

As integrated circuits become more complex, they are embedded in every aspect of critical infrastructure, from power grids to weapon systems. The reliance on foreign manufacturers for these components presents a significant risk in hybrid warfare. Adversaries may introduce backdoors or hidden vulnerabilities into the supply chain, which can be exploited during a conflict. This potential for supply chain manipulation means that hybrid warfare can begin long before hostilities are apparent, with actors planting digital "seeds" that can later be activated to cripple an opponent's infrastructure.

The United States and its allies have recognized the dangers posed by relying on foreign-manufactured integrated circuits and have taken steps to secure their supply chains. However, the sheer complexity of the global semiconductor market makes complete security nearly impossible. This interdependence on global technology markets is a key theme in the evolution of hybrid warfare, where the disruption of IC production or function can become a strategic weapon.

3. Reliance on Electronics in Critical Infrastructure

Modern societies are deeply reliant on electronic systems to maintain everyday life. From traffic control to hospital operations, every sector is powered by digital networks and electronic devices. This reliance is both a strength and a vulnerability. In hybrid warfare, the disruption of critical infrastructure through cyberattacks can have cascading effects that cripple a society's ability to function.

In hybrid conflicts, cyberattacks may be designed to cause chaos by targeting transportation networks, financial institutions, or emergency services. These disruptions may not directly impact military targets, but they weaken the fabric of society, causing panic and undermining public trust in government institutions.

Additionally, the use of electronics in military applications such as drones, satellite systems, and precision-guided munitions makes the defence sector particularly vulnerable to hybrid attacks. Adversaries can exploit weaknesses in communication networks or GPS systems, rendering advanced military hardware ineffective. Thus, the line between civilian and military infrastructure is blurred in hybrid warfare, as both are heavily dependent on interconnected electronic systems.

Known Actors in Hybrid Warfare

Several state actors have emerged as key players in the use and development of hybrid warfare strategies. While non-state actors, such as terrorist organizations, also engage in hybrid tactics, nation-states possess the resources and infrastructure necessary to execute large-scale operations.

1. Russia

Russia is often seen as the archetype of hybrid warfare, particularly due to its strategic use of cyberattacks and disinformation campaigns. Its annexation of Crimea in 2014 is a prime example of hybrid tactics, combining covert military operations with a sustained cyber and propaganda campaign. Russia's use of information warfare spreading disinformation through state-run media and social networks has allowed it to shape public perception both domestically and abroad, undermining Western influence.

In addition to its information operations, Russia has developed sophisticated cyber capabilities. Attacks on Ukraine's power grid in 2015 and 2016 showcased Russia's ability to disrupt critical infrastructure through cyber means. These attacks not only caused widespread power outages but also served as a demonstration of Russia's growing proficiency in combining cyber operations with physical warfare.

2. China

China's approach to hybrid warfare is rooted in its concept of "unrestricted warfare," which emphasizes the use of all available means military, economic, and technological to achieve strategic objectives. Unlike Russia's often brazen and direct cyberattacks, China's cyber activities tend to be more covert, focusing on espionage and the long-term theft of intellectual property.

China's cyber capabilities are among the most advanced in the world, and its hybrid warfare strategy includes a strong emphasis on influencing the technological and economic sectors of its adversaries. By stealing sensitive technology and data, China aims to undermine the economic and military advantages of its rivals while simultaneously boosting its technological development.

In recent years, China has also focused on the manipulation of public opinion, particularly through social media platforms. This tactic is designed to create confusion and weaken the political cohesion of its adversaries, often referred to as "cognitive warfare."

3. Iran

Iran has rapidly developed its hybrid warfare capabilities over the past decade, emerging as a significant player in the Middle East. Its cyber capabilities, while not as advanced as those of Russia or China, have allowed it to launch effective operations against its regional adversaries. Iran has employed cyberattacks to target financial institutions, critical infrastructure, and private entities, intending to cause economic disruption and chaos.

In addition to its cyber capabilities, Iran leverages irregular warfare through proxy groups such as Hezbollah, employing a blend of military and paramilitary operations. This combination of cyber and irregular tactics forms the core of Iran's hybrid warfare strategy, aimed at countering more technologically advanced adversaries like the United States and Israel.

Key Example: The Stuxnet Attack on Iran's Nuclear Program

One of the most significant examples of hybrid warfare in the digital age is the 2010 Stuxnet attack on Iran's nuclear program. Widely believed to be the result of a covert operation by the United States and Israel, Stuxnet was a sophisticated computer worm designed to sabotage Iran's uranium enrichment process.

Stuxnet was a groundbreaking form of cyber warfare. It targeted specific industrial control systems, causing Iran's centrifuges to spin out of control while simultaneously feeding false information to monitoring systems. As a result, Iranian officials were unaware of the damage being done until it was too late. The attack set back Iran's nuclear program for several years without the need for a military strike.

What made Stuxnet particularly notable was its precision. Unlike typical malware, which spreads indiscriminately, Stuxnet was engineered to target specific hardware in a specific facility, showing the potential for cyber weapons to have direct, physical effects. The attack highlighted the growing capabilities of cyber warfare and set the stage for future operations aimed at critical infrastructure.

Conclusion: The Future of Hybrid Warfare

Hybrid warfare represents the convergence of traditional and modern tactics in the digital age. It thrives on exploiting vulnerabilities in cyber systems, critical infrastructure, and the information space, allowing adversaries to achieve strategic objectives without direct military confrontation. As technology continues to evolve, the tools available for hybrid warfare will become more sophisticated, making the defence against these threats increasingly complex.

Nations will need to focus not only on bolstering their military capabilities but also on securing their digital infrastructure and supply chains. In an age where wars may be won or lost in cyberspace, the ability to defend against hybrid attacks will be crucial to national security.

Chapter 2: "EMP: The Silent Weapon"

Overview

In modern warfare, few weapons possess the subtle yet devastating power of an Electromagnetic Pulse (EMP). EMPs are sudden bursts of electromagnetic energy that can arise naturally, such as from solar storms, or be man-made, most commonly through nuclear detonations or specialized EMP weapons. When deployed with precision, they can cripple entire societies without a single human casualty by incapacitating the technological systems upon which those societies depend.

In a world where microchips and digital circuits are the backbone of critical infrastructure power grids, communications, financial institutions, medical services, transportation, and even the military an EMP can devastate a nation's operational ability within seconds. At its most dangerous, an EMP strike can cause cascading failures, rendering everything from household electronics to complex defence networks inoperable.

But how does such a pulse cause this level of destruction? An EMP overloads electrical systems by inducing high levels of current, which in turn can destroy delicate microchips, burn out circuits, and blow fuses. Any technology that relies on these components is vulnerable meaning nearly everything in a modern society is at risk.

Understanding the mechanics and effects of EMPs is vital in recognizing the magnitude of their threat in the digital age, especially as geopolitical tensions rise and several nations actively develop EMP capabilities as part of their arsenal.

Technical Analysis: The Impact of EMP on Different Scales

An EMP's destructive capability is measured by the scale of its deployment. At a localized level, an EMP can disable electronics in a small, defined area taking down power grids, disabling communications, or incapacitating vital military assets. On a broader scale, however, an EMP attack could bring a nation to its knees.

An EMP is divided into three phases based on its effects:

E1: The initial, fast pulse that lasts for a fraction of a second. This phase has the most severe impact on electronics, as it induces high-voltage spikes in circuits, especially affecting microchips and smaller, sensitive devices. In milliseconds, this burst of energy overwhelms any unshielded system, rendering everything from computers to medical equipment inoperative.

E2: A slower phase, similar to natural lightning strikes, which affects larger-scale systems like power grids and communication lines. While less immediately destructive than E1, E2 has a cumulative effect especially if infrastructure has already been compromised by E1.

E3: A final, longer pulse lasting minutes to hours, with effects similar to a geomagnetic storm caused by solar flares. This phase primarily affects large-scale systems like power transformers and electrical grids. Its slower onset targets the nation's most vital energy infrastructure.

At the lowest end, localized EMP attacks can target specific military installations or critical infrastructure, knocking out defence systems or creating confusion in the wake of sudden outages. A well-placed EMP bomb could cause a city's electrical grid to collapse, sending a cascade of failure across regional systems. Even a small, localized EMP event could disrupt commerce, transportation, and emergency services, plunging the area into chaos.

At the other extreme, a high-altitude nuclear EMP (HEMP) could be detonated tens or even hundreds of kilometres above a nation's surface. The blast would not cause physical destruction but would release a massive EMP, covering an area the size of a continent. In such an event, national power grids, satellite communications, and transportation networks could fail simultaneously, effectively plunging entire regions into prolonged darkness and societal breakdown. The national paralysis caused by such an attack would be far-reaching, with the time to recover stretching from months to years, depending on the nation's preparedness.

Historical Reference: Starfish Prime

One of the most illuminating historical examples of the power of an EMP came during the Cold War in the form of a U.S. nuclear test known as Starfish Prime. On July 9, 1962, the United States detonated a 1.4-megaton thermonuclear warhead 400 kilometres above the Pacific Ocean as part of an experimental series of high-altitude nuclear tests. The effects of the explosion were felt far beyond the immediate test area.

Though the test took place over the Pacific, over 1,400 kilometres away in Hawaii, electrical systems were disrupted. Streetlights flickered out, telecommunication services were interrupted, and even the state's radar systems experienced interference. The detonation highlighted the far-reaching consequences of an EMP, even when conducted far from populated areas. Though the infrastructure of the time was far less dependent on microelectronics compared to today, the Starfish Prime test showed the inherent vulnerability of modern systems to such bursts of electromagnetic energy.

More importantly, the test demonstrated that a high-altitude detonation could affect a much broader region than anticipated. The data from Starfish Prime continues to serve as a critical reference point for military and civilian authorities preparing for the possibility of an EMP attack. It also catalyzed further research into EMP resilience and countermeasures though modern advances in technology have also multiplied vulnerabilities.

Known Threats

In the realm of international military strategy, EMP weapons are no longer theoretical they are a growing reality. Some of the world's most prominent military powers have recognized the destructive potential of EMPs and have incorporated this technology into their arsenals, particularly within the framework of hybrid warfare, where non-lethal yet highly effective strikes can paralyze a nation's defence and economic infrastructure.

North Korea: A key player in the development of EMP technology, North Korea has repeatedly emphasized its desire to use nuclear technology in unconventional ways. Intelligence reports and defectors have indicated that North Korea views EMP attacks as a strategic equalizer against technologically superior adversaries like the United States. A missile detonated at a high altitude over South Korea, Japan, or the U.S. could knock out key infrastructure, leaving these nations vulnerable to follow-up attacks or diplomatic concessions.

China: China's military strategy includes sophisticated electronic warfare, and their advancement in EMP research is well documented. The Chinese government has explored both nuclear and non-nuclear EMP weapons, with research pointing to their ability to use EMP strikes to weaken enemy defences before traditional military engagement. In an asymmetric warfare scenario, China could use EMPs to incapacitate a country's digital infrastructure, leaving it vulnerable to cyberattacks, economic sabotage, or even kinetic strikes.

Russia: Long an innovator in electronic and cyber warfare, Russia has continued to develop EMP capabilities, which are seen as part of its broader hybrid warfare tactics. Russia has been accused of testing high-altitude nuclear devices specifically designed to generate EMPs, and it has demonstrated an interest in utilizing such devices as part of its multi-pronged approach to conflict, where cyber, psychological, and physical warfare merge. The Russian military considers EMPs not only as offensive weapons but also as defensive tools, capable of neutralizing enemy electronics during conflict.

These known actors in the EMP arms race, coupled with the increasing sophistication of missile technology, make it clear that the

EMP threat is no longer hypothetical. Nations without adequate shielding or infrastructure resilience risk national catastrophe should they face even a limited EMP attack.

Conclusion

The rise of EMPs as a weapon of choice in modern warfare reflects the broader trend of hybrid warfare attacks designed to inflict maximum damage with minimal kinetic force. As more nations develop EMP capabilities, the world becomes increasingly vulnerable to an invisible, non-lethal, yet highly destructive form of attack. Preparing for and mitigating the effects of EMPs, from localized strikes to large-scale national assaults, should be a priority for governments worldwide, especially those with heavy reliance on digital infrastructure.

Chapter 3: "Sabotage at the Source: Hardware-Level Attacks"

Overview

In the evolving landscape of modern warfare and global espionage, hardware-level attacks represent a critical yet often overlooked vulnerability. Unlike software malware or cyber-intrusions that exploit weaknesses post-production, hardware-level sabotage involves introducing malicious components or functionality directly into the physical makeup of devices microchips, circuits, or other essential parts. These vulnerabilities can be embedded during the manufacturing phase, making detection almost impossible once these components are integrated into larger systems.

The insidious nature of hardware-based attacks lies in their subtlety and long-term potential for disruption. Unlike traditional cyber-attacks that may be neutralized with updates or patches, a compromised microchip or circuit acts as a "kill switch," capable of disabling, degrading, or covertly monitoring an entire system, often without any outward signs of malfunction. These kinds of attacks present a formidable threat to modern military systems, corporate operations, critical infrastructure, and consumer devices alike.

In this chapter, we will explore how these types of attacks can be engineered during the manufacturing process, the strategic players involved in exploiting this vector of attack, and real-world case studies where such vulnerabilities have allegedly compromised global supply chains.

Exploiting Manufacturing Vulnerabilities

The complexity and cost of manufacturing microchips and integrated circuits have driven much of the world's production to regions where labour costs are lower, with China standing as the dominant player. While this has driven down production costs and sped up innovation, it has also opened the door to potential security risks, as foreign manufacturers can tamper with the designs or functionality of chips before they ever leave the factory.

Kill switches are one of the most notorious forms of hardware-level sabotage. These switches are components or instructions built into the circuitry that allows an adversary to remotely disable or degrade the functionality of the chip. Often integrated so seamlessly that they appear as legitimate parts of the design, these switches can be activated through a remote signal or under specific conditions, creating a latent threat that can be triggered at a time of strategic advantage.

Another common method of hardware sabotage is the insertion of **backdoor access points** directly into the chip. These backdoors allow an attacker to secretly control or monitor the functions of a device without detection by software-based security systems. Once a chip is in a critical system such as a communications satellite, a server farm, or a military drone the attacker can access classified data, shut down operations, or reprogram devices to operate according to their agenda.

While both kill switches and backdoors can be introduced at the design stage, the complexity of modern chips and the global distribution of their production make it extremely difficult to vet every component for these types of threats. This has created an environment where nation-states and other actors with the resources to infiltrate the supply chain can embed malicious hardware into devices that will be distributed globally.

China: The Dominant Player in Chip Manufacturing

China's role as the world's largest producer of microchips and integrated circuits places it at the centre of any discussion on hardware-level attacks. With approximately 75% of global chip manufacturing concentrated in East Asia, China holds a significant portion of that market share, giving it potential access to countless supply chains.

Though these chips often find their way into consumer devices like smartphones and laptops, they are also essential components in military systems, financial networks, and government communications. The potential for a state actor like China to exploit this dominance in chip manufacturing has been a source of concern for many Western governments and companies. Despite regulatory efforts to ensure the security of technology imports, it remains nearly impossible to guarantee that every component produced in foreign factories is free from tampering.

China's deep involvement in global manufacturing also means that it could potentially leverage the sheer volume of its exports to infiltrate a wide array of systems simultaneously. Whether acting through state-sponsored espionage or contracted private entities, China can embed kill switches or backdoors into the vast array of devices it produces for the global market.

Case Study: The Supermicro Hack Allegations

In 2018, one of the most alarming reports of hardware-level sabotage emerged involving Supermicro, a major supplier of server motherboards. According to an explosive report by Bloomberg, tiny microchips about the size of a grain of rice were allegedly found embedded into Supermicro's server motherboards during the manufacturing process. These chips, which were not part of the original design, allegedly provided backdoor access to anyone with knowledge of their presence and how to exploit them. The motherboards were used by major corporations, including Apple and Amazon, as well as government contractors and other high-profile organizations, potentially compromising vast amounts of sensitive data.

The attack was described as a sophisticated, supply-chain manipulation orchestrated by operatives linked to the Chinese military. While China has denied involvement and the companies implicated in the report have either downplayed or denied the findings, the Supermicro case has continued to spark significant concern about the vulnerabilities inherent in outsourcing technology manufacturing to foreign entities.

The scale and scope of the alleged Supermicro hack illustrate just how dangerous hardware-level attacks can be. Unlike software vulnerabilities, which are relatively straightforward to patch once discovered, compromised hardware is much harder to detect and almost impossible to remove without replacing the physical components. In systems as complex and widespread as those in global corporations like Amazon and Apple, detecting these chips would require detailed, invasive scrutiny of every device, a process that could take years.

The Supermicro case was particularly worrying because of the potential national security implications. If the allegations were true, China could have used this access to monitor and manipulate servers used by some of the world's largest tech companies and, by extension, critical infrastructure. While the full truth of the situation remains contested, the case remains a critical example of the risks posed by hardware-level sabotage.

Implications for the Future

As global reliance on microchips continues to grow, the potential for hardware-based attacks will only increase. Whether through kill switches, backdoor access, or other forms of physical tampering, the risk of hardware sabotage must be considered a key element of modern cybersecurity strategies.

Countries that rely heavily on foreign-manufactured technology, particularly for critical infrastructure and military systems, face an inherent vulnerability. The complexity of these systems makes it nearly impossible to monitor every component, and as attacks become more sophisticated, the lines between legitimate components and malicious alterations will blur further.

Efforts to build secure supply chains will likely require a combination of technical innovation, rigorous testing standards, and increased domestic production of critical technologies. Governments may also impose stricter regulations on technology imports, requiring thorough vetting processes to mitigate the risk of compromised components.

Conclusion

Hardware-level sabotage poses one of the most formidable challenges in modern hybrid warfare. Unlike software-based attacks that can be rapidly identified and neutralized, physical tampering at the production stage is nearly invisible until it is too late. China's dominance in chip manufacturing and the increasing complexity of global supply chains have made this threat not only possible but highly probable. As the Supermicro case demonstrates, the consequences of compromised hardware can be severe, affecting everything from corporate security to national defence. To mitigate this growing risk, nations must develop comprehensive strategies to protect their supply chains and safeguard critical infrastructure from sabotage at the source.

Chapter 4: Malicious Code: Digital Sabotage in a Connected World

Overview: Digital Sabotage in a Connected World

As modern societies continue to integrate advanced digital technologies into their infrastructure, the potential for malicious code to wreak havoc has become increasingly dire. Malicious software and firmware attacks have evolved beyond simple data theft or system damage; today, they can compromise the very foundation of hardware systems, microchips, and integrated circuits, which are at the heart of global communication, security, and commerce.

Microchips tiny silicon circuits that power everything from smartphones to military satellites are the core infrastructure of the digital age. Malicious actors have developed increasingly sophisticated means of compromising these devices, inserting backdoors, and creating vulnerabilities that can remain undetected for years. Firmware attacks, which specifically target the embedded code controlling hardware, have become a weapon of choice for state-sponsored groups and cybercriminal organizations alike, enabling them to bypass traditional security measures. By compromising the software and firmware layers that manage these chips, attackers gain unprecedented access to the systems they govern, enabling cyber espionage, sabotage, and large-scale disruption.

What makes these attacks particularly insidious is their covert nature. Unlike a malware attack that disrupts operations in real-time, malicious code introduced into firmware or microchips can lie dormant, awaiting activation. Once triggered, these backdoors can be used to extract sensitive data, cripple systems, or initiate further attacks. The scale of such sabotage is magnified by the increasingly interconnected nature of global infrastructure, where a single compromised device could serve as the entry point for a cascade of devastating intrusions.

Mechanisms: The Introduction of Malware into Critical Systems

The insertion of malware into critical systems is often accomplished through several vectors, each of which exploits different vulnerabilities. Ransomware, for example, encrypts critical data and systems, demanding payment for their release, while targeted malware can manipulate system operations or siphon off sensitive information without alerting the victim. However, cybercriminals and state-sponsored actors have developed far more subtle and sophisticated methods of digital sabotage.

1. **Firmware Exploits:** Firmware is a specialized form of software that manages hardware components, and its low-level nature makes it an attractive target for attackers. The malware injected into firmware can control devices before the operating system even boots, allowing attackers to bypass most conventional security protocols. Since firmware is rarely updated or closely monitored, vulnerabilities can persist for long periods.

2. **Supply Chain Infiltration:** Similar to hardware-based sabotage discussed in Chapter 3, cyber saboteurs exploit supply chain weaknesses by embedding malicious code at various stages of production or software development. The complexity of global supply chains, with numerous third-party vendors and subcontractors, provides ample opportunity for attackers to introduce vulnerabilities that go unnoticed until it is too late.

3. **Zero-Day Exploits:** A particularly dangerous category of cyber attack, zero-day exploits target vulnerabilities that are unknown to the system's developers and security teams. This means that defences are unprepared for the attack, allowing malicious code to take root before any countermeasures can be deployed. Zero-day attacks, often used by state-sponsored groups, can have far-reaching effects, as was seen in the famous Stuxnet attack covered in Chapter 1.

4. **Ransomware as a Tool for Sabotage:** While ransomware is
    often viewed as a means of extortion, its potential for systemic
    sabotage cannot be understated. By encrypting critical systems
    and data, ransomware can grind entire businesses and
    industries to a halt. In the context of national infrastructure,
    such attacks could result in catastrophic failures, from the
    collapse of financial systems to the disruption of healthcare
    services.

The covert nature of these intrusions is often what makes them so
effective. Attackers may lay the groundwork years in advance, patiently
waiting for the right moment to strike. Once activated, these intrusions
can manipulate systems in ways that are difficult, if not impossible, to
reverse.

Historical Case: The SolarWinds Breach and Its Global Effects
One of the most infamous and far-reaching examples of digital
sabotage in the modern age is the SolarWinds breach, a cyber-attack
that sent shockwaves through governments, corporations, and global
security communities in 2020. The attack began with the introduction
of malicious code into the software updates of SolarWinds, a major
provider of IT management software whose products were used by
thousands of organizations worldwide, including numerous branches of
the U.S. government.

The attack was remarkable not only for its technical complexity but
also for the scale of its impact. The hackers believed to be part of a
Russian state-sponsored group, exploited weaknesses in SolarWinds'
Orion software, compromising its update mechanism to distribute
malware to the company's clients. Once deployed, the malware provided
attackers with remote access to the infected systems, allowing them to
conduct espionage, steal sensitive information, and potentially set the
stage for future attacks.

The fallout from the SolarWinds breach was global in scope, affecting over 18,000 organizations, including critical government agencies such as the U.S. Department of Homeland Security, the Department of Defence, and the Treasury Department. Beyond the immediate theft of sensitive information, the breach raised alarms about the vulnerability of software supply chains, which had been seen as largely secure. It also illustrated the potential for long-term sabotage, as some experts speculated that the attackers could use the compromised systems as platforms for future attacks.

The SolarWinds breach serves as a sobering reminder of the extent to which malicious actors can exploit even well-established companies, compromising critical infrastructure on a global scale. It also demonstrated that even the most secure systems can fall prey to sophisticated, well-resourced cyber attacks, laying the groundwork for similar future operations.

Known Actors: Russia's Fancy Bear and China's PLA Unit 61398

Among the many cyber groups capable of launching sophisticated digital sabotage campaigns, two have gained particular notoriety: Russia's Fancy Bear and China's PLA Unit 61398.

1. **Fancy Bear (APT28):** Fancy Bear is a Russian cyber espionage group that has been linked to numerous high-profile cyber attacks, including the 2016 Democratic National Committee email breach in the United States and various campaigns targeting NATO, Eastern European governments, and defence contractors. Believed to be associated with Russia's GRU (military intelligence), Fancy Bear's operations often involve spear-phishing campaigns, exploiting zero-day vulnerabilities, and inserting malware into systems to exfiltrate sensitive information or disrupt operations. Their extensive experience in cyber sabotage makes them one of the most dangerous and effective state-sponsored groups in existence.

2. **PLA Unit 61398:** China's People's Liberation Army Unit 61398 has been identified as one of the primary actors behind China's cyber-espionage and cyber-sabotage activities. This unit has been implicated in numerous cyber attacks aimed at stealing intellectual property, military secrets, and confidential government information from Western targets. Unlike Fancy Bear, which focuses heavily on political disruption, PLA Unit 61398 tends to target economic and industrial secrets, using sophisticated cyber tactics to infiltrate corporate networks and government systems. The group's activities are often intertwined with China's broader geopolitical objectives, as they seek to gain economic and technological advantages over their rivals.

Both Fancy Bear and PLA Unit 61398 are emblematic of a broader trend in cyber warfare, where state-sponsored groups target critical infrastructure, corporations, and government systems as part of long-term sabotage campaigns. Their operations are designed to go unnoticed for as long as possible, allowing them to extract valuable information or insert backdoors into systems that can be exploited at a later date.

In summary, digital sabotage through malicious code represents one of the most pressing security challenges of the modern era. The covert nature of these attacks, combined with the growing complexity and interdependence of global infrastructure, means that a single intrusion can have catastrophic ripple effects. The examples of the SolarWinds breach, Fancy Bear, and PLA Unit 61398 underscore the sheer scale and sophistication of the threat, reminding us that in a world driven by digital connections, the next act of sabotage could already be unfolding, undetected.

Chapter 5: The Threat of Supply Chain Compromise

Overview

In the interconnected, globalized economy of the 21st century, the supply chain of electronic components has become a web of dependency that spans continents. This globalization brings efficiencies and reduced costs but also presents a new realm of vulnerability, particularly in sectors that are vital to national security and critical infrastructure. The introduction of compromised technology be it hardware or software into sensitive systems poses a significant risk. Unlike traditional attacks, a supply chain compromise can operate undetected for years, eroding security at its very foundation.

The threat of supply chain compromise is not speculative. Recent history has shown how vulnerable our systems are to malicious actors infiltrating the manufacturing, distribution, and even maintenance processes of critical technologies. With the rise of hybrid warfare, as discussed in *Chapter 1*, these compromises are becoming part of a broader strategy by state and non-state actors alike. Unlike overt military aggression, these compromises are covert, and systemic, and can be catastrophic when activated at a critical juncture. This chapter delves into the specific vulnerabilities of key sectors and the known actors, namely Russia and China, who have systematically exploited these weaknesses to further their geopolitical ambitions.

Vulnerable Sectors

1. **defence** The defence sector is one of the most targeted in terms of supply chain compromise. Modern military systems rely heavily on sophisticated electronics, from guidance systems in missiles to communication networks and advanced computing in fighter jets. The dependency on these technologies makes defence operations particularly susceptible to manipulation or

sabotage if compromised components are introduced at any point in the supply chain.

The integration of foreign-manufactured microchips and other components into weapons systems can open the door to catastrophic failures or even direct enemy control in the event of a conflict. A compromised radar system or the failure of an unmanned aerial vehicle could decisively tilt the balance in a confrontation. Moreover, given the long life cycles of military technologies, the effects of supply chain infiltration could be latent, waiting to manifest during a crucial moment.

1. **Aerospace** Aerospace systems, both civilian and military, are heavily dependent on highly specialized electronics. These range from navigation and communication systems to sensors used for intelligence gathering and threat detection. Sabotage in aerospace could lead to communication blackouts, faulty satellite data, or even the disablement of space-based defence mechanisms.

In a world where space is increasingly militarized, control over satellite infrastructure can offer significant strategic advantages. As mentioned in *Chapter 3*, where hardware-level attacks on microchips were discussed, a similar risk exists within the aerospace industry, where subtle sabotage at the manufacturing stage can render essential components vulnerable.

1. **Healthcare** infrastructure is particularly vulnerable due to its reliance on interconnected systems, from patient databases to life-support equipment. The growth of telemedicine and the digitization of medical records has exposed hospitals and healthcare networks to cyber attacks, but a supply chain compromise could go beyond mere data theft. Sabotaged equipment could lead to malfunctioning diagnostic machines

or compromised pharmaceutical production processes.

In an era of increasing dependency on technology for life-saving operations, healthcare has become a prime target. As seen in *Chapter 4*, where malicious software compromises were explored, the introduction of corrupted firmware or hardware into medical equipment can lead to life-threatening consequences, either through malfunction or ransomware-style extortion.

1. **Telecommunications** Telecommunications infrastructure, especially with the global rollout of 5G networks, is a critical backbone for national security, economic activity, and civilian communication. A compromised supply chain in this sector could allow adversaries to intercept communications, introduce malware, or even bring entire networks offline.

The infiltration of telecommunications infrastructure by adversaries like China and Russia is well-documented. For example, concerns over China's Huawei equipment in 5G networks highlight how supply chain compromise is a modern battlefield in digital warfare. These actions can not only affect domestic communications but also compromise international diplomatic channels and military communication systems.

Known Actors: Russian and Chinese Infiltration

Two of the most prominent actors in the domain of supply chain compromise are Russia and China. Both nations have well-documented histories of infiltrating critical infrastructure supply chains as part of broader hybrid warfare strategies.

1. **China** China's dominance in the manufacturing of electronics, particularly microchips, places it in a unique position of power in the global supply chain. As explored in *Chapter 3*, China's role as a leading chip manufacturer is a double-edged sword. On one hand, the world benefits from the cost-effective

production of high-quality electronics; on the other, China can insert malicious components into the hardware it exports.

The infamous Supermicro hack, discussed in previous chapters, demonstrated China's potential to infiltrate the very heart of Western technological infrastructure. By embedding a tiny microchip into Supermicro motherboards, it was able to access sensitive data from companies like Apple and Amazon. Although Beijing has denied involvement, these allegations continue to raise concerns over China's long-term intentions and its capability to use supply chain compromise as a tool for geopolitical dominance.

China's People's Liberation Army (PLA) is often associated with cyber-espionage campaigns, as detailed in *Chapter 4*, such as those conducted by Unit 61398. But beyond cyber-attacks, China's strategy of embedding itself in the global supply chain gives it a potent, covert weapon. If necessary, China could remotely disable or manipulate technologies used by its adversaries. This extends to defence systems, communications, and even civilian infrastructure, making it a formidable threat in the sphere of hybrid warfare.

1. **Russia** Russia, like China, has been deeply involved in infiltrating supply chains, especially those critical to Western defence and intelligence infrastructures. Russian groups, such as Fancy Bear, known for their involvement in cyber-espionage (Chapter 4), have taken an aggressive approach towards supply chain compromise. Rather than focus solely on hardware, Russian actors frequently combine cyber intrusions with physical sabotage of supply chains, blending digital and traditional espionage.

The SolarWinds breach, discussed in detail in *Chapter 4*, is a stark example of Russia's capabilities in this domain. By compromising SolarWinds, a widely-used IT management software, Russian hackers gained access to the networks of countless government and private sector organizations globally. This attack demonstrated how a well-executed supply chain compromise can have a ripple effect, creating vulnerabilities across multiple sectors at once, with potentially devastating results.

Russia's doctrine of hybrid warfare, much like China's, relies on exploiting systemic weaknesses in the infrastructure of its adversaries. Supply chains, being dispersed and often difficult to secure, present a prime target for Russia's tactics of asymmetrical warfare.

Conclusion

As technology becomes ever more embedded in our critical infrastructure, the threat of supply chain compromise grows more urgent. Unlike overt forms of warfare, this form of sabotage is insidious, often lying dormant until activated at a critical moment. The sectors most vulnerable defence, aerospace, healthcare, and telecommunications form the very foundation of modern society, and the consequences of compromise in these areas could be catastrophic.

Russia and China have already demonstrated their willingness and capability to infiltrate supply chains as part of their broader hybrid warfare strategies. The lessons from previous chapters show how malicious software, firmware, and hardware can be inserted into systems without detection, creating long-term vulnerabilities. The onus now falls on policymakers, companies, and security agencies to ensure that supply chains are secured. This means not only defending against the digital threats of malware and ransomware but also ensuring that physical components often produced halfway around the world are free from hidden sabotage.

As hybrid warfare evolves, so too must our strategies for securing supply chains. The next major conflict may not begin with bombs or missiles but with the subtle activation of a long-planted compromise in the very electronics that drive our world.

Chapter 6: Critical Infrastructure Under Siege: Power Grids and Beyond

Overview: The Vulnerability of National Power Grids and Critical Infrastructure to Attacks on Embedded Systems

In the modern world, the electrical grid is the backbone of a nation's critical infrastructure. It powers homes, businesses, hospitals, transportation, and communication networks. However, as power grids become more sophisticated and interconnected through technologies like smart grids and the integration of renewable energy sources, they also become more vulnerable to malicious attacks. At the core of this vulnerability is the embedded technology software, hardware, and firmware that governs these systems. From small-scale local grids to vast national networks, the complexity of the digital infrastructure that underpins power generation and distribution has opened up new avenues for cyber sabotage.

Embedded systems are at the heart of the grid's operations, enabling remote monitoring, load balancing, and the maintenance of infrastructure. However, these same systems, if compromised, can serve as entry points for attackers to disrupt electricity supply and cause widespread chaos. In a world where energy is the lifeblood of a modern economy, an attack on the grid could lead to cascading failures across multiple sectors, from healthcare to defence. This chapter delves into the vulnerabilities of these embedded systems, the key technologies that both protect and threaten them and the potential consequences of a successful attack on critical infrastructure.

Key Technologies: Smart Grids and SCADA Systems

Two of the most vital technologies that have transformed the modern grid are **smart grids** and **SCADA (Supervisory Control and Data Acquisition) systems**. Smart grids allow for real-time monitoring, dynamic load management, and the integration of distributed energy sources like wind and solar. They also enable consumers to play a more active role in managing their energy consumption. However, the interconnectivity that makes smart grids more efficient also makes them more vulnerable to cyberattacks. Each sensor, meter, and connected device within the smart grid represents a potential entry point for a determined adversary.

SCADA systems, meanwhile, are critical to controlling and monitoring industrial processes. Found in power plants, water treatment facilities, and gas pipelines, SCADA systems are often referred to as the "nervous system" of critical infrastructure. These systems allow operators to monitor and control vast, complex networks from a central location. However, many SCADA systems were designed in an era when cybersecurity was not a primary concern, leaving them exposed to modern-day threats.

As Chapter 4 outlined in discussing malicious code, SCADA systems are particularly susceptible to malware and ransomware attacks. An adversary that gains access to a SCADA network could manipulate system parameters, shut down critical operations, or introduce catastrophic failures in real-time. In the context of power grids, this could lead to widespread blackouts or even damage to physical infrastructure, such as transformers and substations, resulting in prolonged outages that could take weeks to repair.

Historical Case: Russia's Cyberattacks on Ukraine's Power Grid (2015, 2016)

One of the most significant examples of a cyberattack on a national power grid occurred in Ukraine in 2015 and again in 2016. In December 2015, a sophisticated cyberattack disabled three of Ukraine's regional power distribution companies, cutting power to approximately 225,000 people for several hours. The attackers had gained access to the power grid months before, using spear-phishing emails to target employees and install malware that allowed them to gain control of SCADA systems.

Once inside, they remotely shut down power substations, rendering them inoperable.

In 2016, Ukraine suffered a second, even more advanced attack, which affected the power distribution network in Kyiv. This attack was particularly notable because it involved the use of highly specialized malware called **Industroyer**, which was designed specifically to target industrial control systems. Industroyer was capable of communicating with various industrial protocols used in energy systems and could be programmed to issue commands that would disable critical infrastructure.

Both of these attacks are widely believed to have been carried out by **Russian state-sponsored groups**, further highlighting the role of cyber warfare in modern geopolitical conflicts. The Ukrainian case demonstrates how vulnerable national power grids are to cyberattacks and serves as a warning of the potential for even more destructive incidents in the future. While Ukraine managed to restore power relatively quickly, a more coordinated or widespread attack could result in far longer outages, particularly if it targeted multiple regions or vital infrastructure simultaneously.

Potential Consequences: Power Outages, Breakdown of Transportation, and Loss of Communication Networks

A successful attack on a national power grid would have catastrophic consequences that extend far beyond the immediate loss of electricity. Modern societies are deeply interconnected, with multiple sectors relying on continuous, reliable access to power. If the electrical grid were to be disabled for an extended period, the following consequences could unfold:

1. **Power Outages**: Extended blackouts would not only inconvenience citizens but could also lead to a breakdown in essential services. Hospitals, which rely on stable electricity to run life-saving equipment, would be forced to switch to backup

generators. Water and sewage systems could fail, leading to sanitation crises. In colder climates, heating systems would shut down, creating dangerous conditions for residents.

2. **Breakdown of Transportation**: Modern transportation systems are heavily reliant on electricity. Trains, subways, and electric vehicle charging stations would all be rendered inoperable. Traffic control systems, including lights and sensors, would fail, leading to chaos on the roads. Airports, which rely on extensive computer networks to manage air traffic, could also be severely disrupted, leading to the grounding of flights.

3. **Loss of Communication Networks**: The loss of electricity would disable communication networks, including cell towers, internet service providers, and data centres. In a prolonged blackout, backup systems would eventually fail, cutting off both civilian and government communication channels. This loss of connectivity would severely hinder any efforts to coordinate a response to the crisis.

These cascading failures highlight the interdependence of modern infrastructure. An attack on the power grid is not merely an isolated event but a catalyst for widespread disruption across multiple sectors. As demonstrated in previous chapters, the globalized supply chain (Chapter 5), embedded vulnerabilities in hardware (Chapter 3), and the use of malware (Chapter 4) create multiple avenues for cyber sabotage that extend well beyond a single target. Power grids are simply one of the most visible and immediate targets, but an attack here can reverberate across society in unpredictable and far-reaching ways.

Resilience and Response

In response to these growing threats, many nations have begun investing in the resilience of their critical infrastructure. However, as highlighted in the discussion of hybrid warfare in Chapter 1, these efforts are often reactive rather than proactive. Power grids are increasingly being segmented to prevent the spread of an attack, and newer SCADA systems are being designed with cybersecurity in mind. Nevertheless, the sheer size and complexity of national grids, coupled with the presence of outdated technology in many regions, means that vulnerabilities will continue to exist for the foreseeable future.

The lessons from Ukraine demonstrate the importance of preparation. Nations must invest not only in defensive measures but also in redundancy and recovery strategies. In the event of an attack, the ability to restore power quickly and safely will be crucial to preventing broader societal collapse.

As we move forward into an era of **smart infrastructure**, the need for secure and resilient embedded systems will only grow. Whether through cyberattacks or the insertion of malicious code during the manufacturing process, the siege on critical infrastructure is one of the most pressing security challenges of our time. It is not a question of *if* an attack will occur but rather *when* and how well-prepared nations will be to respond when it does.

Conclusion

Critical infrastructure, particularly power grids, represents a prime target in the landscape of modern cyber warfare. As we've seen in historical cases such as the Ukraine attacks, the integration of digital technologies into these systems has increased their vulnerability. The consequences of a successful cyberattack on a power grid are profound, with far-reaching implications for national security, economic stability, and public health. This chapter underscores the importance of proactive cybersecurity measures, collaboration between governments and industry, and the continual adaptation of strategies to defend against evolving threats.

In an interconnected world, the protection of power grids and other critical infrastructure is a matter of national survival. Each system, whether a SCADA network or a smart grid, must be hardened against the onslaught of cyber warfare, lest we face the devastating reality of a nation plunged into darkness.

Chapter 7: A Nation at Risk: Civilian Impacts of a Chip-Based Attack

Overview: Societal Impacts of Chip-Level Sabotage and EMP Strikes

In today's world, the microchip a nearly invisible component buried within every aspect of modern life has become the linchpin of national infrastructure. From power grids and transportation systems to healthcare, financial networks, and emergency services, these tiny integrated circuits dictate the operation of modern societies. As the complexity of these systems grows, so does their vulnerability to chip-level sabotage and Electromagnetic Pulse (EMP) strikes, forms of attack that can cripple entire nations without firing a single shot in a traditional sense.

Civilian life would be the most vulnerable target in such an attack. In an instant, power could vanish, communication systems could fail, and basic services like water distribution, healthcare, and emergency response could become inoperable. Chip-based sabotage whether through hidden vulnerabilities, malicious code, or hardware manipulation could paralyze essential systems with precision, leaving millions stranded in cities and rural areas alike, unable to access even the most basic resources.

EMP strikes, on the other hand, are even more terrifying. Delivered via nuclear warheads detonated in the upper atmosphere, EMPs can generate vast fields of electromagnetic energy that fry electronics over entire regions. These strikes are not limited to disabling specific systems; rather, they target the entire technological framework upon which modern life depends. While no visible damage might be seen, the consequences could be far-reaching and long-lasting.

Long-Term Effects: Economic Collapse, Famine, and Public Health Crises

The aftermath of a successful chip-based attack or EMP strike would be devastating in both the short and long term. The modern economy, so reliant on digital infrastructure and real-time global transactions, would come to a halt. Financial systems based on electronic transactions would fail, stock markets would collapse, and industries reliant on supply chains and communication would be rendered inoperable. The just-in-time delivery systems that supply major cities with food and essential goods would break down, leading to widespread shortages and the rapid onset of famine, especially in densely populated urban centres.

Without functioning transportation and communication networks, the delivery of essential goods like food, fuel, and medicine would slow to a trickle, if not cease altogether. Supermarkets would quickly be emptied, and as supply lines fail, panic and civil unrest would follow. This scarcity of essential resources could result in food riots and mass migrations out of cities, further compounding the chaos.

The health sector would be among the hardest hit. Hospitals, reliant on uninterrupted power and digital records to manage patients, would be unable to function. Without refrigeration, medications and vaccines would spoil. Life-saving treatments, such as dialysis or surgeries, would become impossible, leading to a sharp increase in mortality. Moreover, public health crises would arise as waste management systems fail, clean water becomes inaccessible, and diseases spread in the absence of medical infrastructure.

The long-term consequences of such attacks extend beyond the physical. Economic collapse and the paralysis of key industries would leave millions unemployed. As government services grind to a halt, the social fabric could unravel. Law enforcement, already overwhelmed, would struggle to maintain order in the face of looting, violence, and mass unrest. Over time, the societal damage would erode the state's ability to respond effectively, leaving the nation in a prolonged state of emergency.

Risk Scenarios: Cascading Effects from Large-Scale Blackouts

One of the most immediate effects of a chip-based attack or EMP strike would be widespread and prolonged blackouts. As detailed in *Chapter 6: Critical Infrastructure Under Siege: Power Grids and Beyond*, power grids are especially vulnerable to both cyberattacks and physical sabotage. A targeted strike against embedded systems could induce long-lasting blackouts, disabling electricity in cities and regions for extended periods.

The collapse of power grids would trigger cascading failures across all sectors of society. Without power, communication networks would shut down, making coordination between emergency services and civilians impossible. Hospitals would cease to function, transportation systems would grind to a halt, and water purification plants would shut off, leaving millions without access to safe drinking water.

A blackout of this magnitude would create a humanitarian crisis within days. As cities plunged into darkness, food supplies would dwindle, leaving urban areas vulnerable to famine. Fuel supplies would be disrupted, making it impossible for emergency responders to reach those in need.

The economic impacts would be equally severe. Without power, manufacturing plants would shut down, industries would stall, and trade would come to a halt. In *Chapter 5: The Threat of Supply Chain Compromise*, we explored how even minor disruptions to supply chains can have far-reaching consequences. A blackout exacerbated by chip-based sabotage would ripple through global markets, halting the production and delivery of essential goods and destabilizing economies around the world.

Beyond the immediate societal collapse, there is an even greater and more existential threat: the potential for nuclear-armed retaliation. If the nation targeted by a chip-based attack or EMP strike possesses nuclear weapons, the inability to differentiate between a conventional or nuclear attack on infrastructure could prompt an extreme defensive response. **In a moment of crisis, where communications have failed and the** scale of the damage is unclear, the attacked nation may interpret the assault as a precursor to a larger-scale military offensive. This uncertainty increases the risk of a retaliatory nuclear strike, leading to global devastation.

The devastation wrought by an EMP or cyber-attack may cripple not only the nation's infrastructure but also its ability to manage its defence systems. The targeted nation, overwhelmed by chaos and lacking real-time intelligence, might be forced to make high-stakes decisions under pressure, misinterpreting the source or intent of the attack. Should a miscalculation occur, a nuclear retaliation could lead to the annihilation of entire cities, further escalating a conflict that started in the digital realm.

Cascading Failures and the Global Context

As discussed in *Chapter 4: Malicious Code: Digital Sabotage in a Connected World*, cyberattacks on critical systems can have a global impact. The same holds for a chip-based attack or EMP strike. The interconnectedness of modern economies means that the collapse of one nation's infrastructure could trigger a chain reaction across international markets. Global supply chains, already vulnerable, would disintegrate, causing shortages of essential goods like food, medicine, and raw materials. Stock markets around the world would plummet, sending global economies into a recession, or worse, a depression.

The geopolitical consequences of such an attack would also be profound. As detailed in *Chapter 1: Introduction to Hybrid Warfare in the Digital Age*, hybrid warfare strategies seek to exploit the vulnerabilities of target nations through a combination of conventional, irregular, and cyber tactics. In the aftermath of a chip-based attack or EMP strike, adversarial nations could exploit the ensuing chaos to advance their geopolitical interests, either by launching military invasions or by destabilizing regional alliances.

Moreover, a power vacuum created by the collapse of a major nation's infrastructure would invite opportunistic actions from non-state actors, such as terrorist organizations and criminal syndicates, seeking to exploit the lawlessness that would follow.

The Unseen Threat: EMP Strikes and Their Silent Devastation

An EMP strike, especially one delivered by a nuclear warhead, would introduce an entirely new level of destruction. As explored in *Chapter 2: EMP: The Silent Weapon*, EMPs generate an electromagnetic burst capable of incapacitating all unshielded electronic devices over a wide area. From power plants to personal devices, everything relying on integrated circuits would be rendered inoperable in seconds.

A high-altitude EMP strike could disable the electronics over an entire continent, plunging vast regions into darkness. The damage from such an attack would be irreversible in the short term, with recovery efforts hampered by the sheer scale of the destruction. Unlike conventional warfare, there would be no immediate visual destruction, but the societal collapse would be near-total.

As discussed, **nuclear-armed states may view an EMP strike as an act of war, potentially prompting them to retaliate with nuclear force.** The resulting escalation could spiral into full-scale nuclear conflict, threatening global security.

Conclusion: A Nation on the Brink of Catastrophe

In a world deeply reliant on embedded electronics and digital infrastructure, the risks posed by chip-based attacks and EMP strikes are both tangible and devastating. From the collapse of civilian services to the threat of nuclear retaliation, the consequences of such an attack would be far-reaching. Nations stand on the brink of catastrophe, with inadequate preparation for the silent and unseen threats that could bring their societies to the edge of collapse.

The potential for a retaliatory nuclear strike highlights the gravity of the situation, underscoring the need for immediate action. Safeguarding critical infrastructure, developing robust contingency plans, and reinforcing diplomatic channels to prevent miscalculation are paramount to ensuring that a chip-based or EMP strike does not trigger an irreversible chain of destruction.

The question remains: are we prepared to protect ourselves from the unseen dangers lurking within the very technology that powers our world? The time to act is now before the silence of an EMP strike or the invisible sabotage of a microchip becomes the defining moment of modern history.

Chapter 8: Hostile Intent: Profiles of Known Bad Actors

Overview

In the globalized and interconnected world of the 21st century, nations and non-state actors alike have come to realize that domination of the digital domain is as crucial as air or sea superiority. Cyber warfare, digital sabotage, and hardware manipulation have become modern battlefields where offensive operations can be carried out without a single shot being fired. As this evolution continues, the capacity to infiltrate, manipulate, or destroy vital technologies including microchips and circuits has become a central element of statecraft and warfare.

This chapter examines the key players, state and non-state, that are not only capable but also motivated to engage in digital warfare. With technical expertise and hostile intent, these actors have actively sought to compromise systems and infrastructures, threatening national security, economic stability, and the integrity of global supply chains.

Russia: Masters of Cyber Warfare and EMP Development

Russia stands at the forefront of digital subversion, with decades of expertise in cyber warfare and an acute understanding of the vulnerabilities inherent in Western infrastructure. Known for its sophisticated cyber-espionage units like *Fancy Bear* (APT28) and *Cozy Bear* (APT29), Russia has not only engaged in extensive cyber theft but has also actively sabotaged critical systems through malware and hardware manipulation. Their attack on Ukraine's power grid in 2015 and 2016, mentioned in Chapter 6, demonstrated their capacity to disrupt national infrastructure through a combination of malware and cyber-enabled sabotage.

More worrisome than purely digital operations, however, is Russia's robust development of electromagnetic pulse (EMP) technology. As discussed in Chapter 2, an EMP attack has the potential to cripple a nation's electrical infrastructure in a matter of seconds by permanently disabling electronics. Russia's experience with nuclear-tipped warheads capable of delivering EMPs means they possess a potentially devastating weapon in the hybrid warfare arsenal. Russian doctrines explicitly include EMP attacks as part of their "first-strike" capabilities, capable of disabling an enemy's command and control systems, communication networks, and critical infrastructure at the onset of a conflict.

Russia's approach blends traditional military aggression with cyber warfare and EMP capabilities, creating a multidimensional threat. They have shown a clear willingness to test their capabilities in real-world scenarios, repeatedly targeting countries like Ukraine, Georgia, and Estonia, using hybrid tactics designed to cause maximum disruption with minimal confrontation.

China: The Silent Dominator of the Tech Supply Chain

China's technological dominance is, in many ways, more subtle yet equally as dangerous as Russia's overt cyber aggression. As discussed extensively in previous chapters, particularly Chapter 3 and Chapter 5, China's strength lies in its overwhelming control over the global electronics supply chain. Responsible for manufacturing vast quantities of microchips, circuits, and hardware used in nearly all modern technology, China's potential for inserting malicious hardware or firmware at the production stage is profound.

One of the most striking examples of potential sabotage at the hardware level was the Supermicro hack, which affected major U.S. corporations like Apple and Amazon. Allegations arose that tiny chips, capable of remote control, were embedded in the hardware of servers, effectively creating a backdoor into some of the world's most secure systems. Though vehemently denied by China, the case underscores the enormous risk inherent in relying on a single nation's supply chain for critical components.

Beyond hardware sabotage, China's commitment to digital espionage is unparalleled. The notorious *PLA Unit 61398*, discussed in

Chapter 4, has been linked to widespread cyber-espionage campaigns targeting defence contractors, government agencies, and critical infrastructure worldwide. Through the use of sophisticated malware, ransomware, and phishing techniques, China has acquired classified information on a scale rivalled only by Russia. The Chinese government's integration of state and corporate sectors also facilitates these efforts, allowing Chinese technology giants to serve as conduits for intelligence gathering and sabotage under the guise of legitimate business operations.

In terms of military and national strategy, China views cyber and supply chain manipulation as essential tools in its broader goal of geopolitical dominance. This is particularly evident in their *Made in China 2025* initiative, which seeks to cement the nation's leadership in critical technologies such as artificial intelligence, 5G networks, and quantum computing. By controlling the production and development of these technologies, China not only gains an economic advantage but also a strategic one, enabling the potential for massive sabotage of foreign technologies embedded with hidden vulnerabilities.

Iran and North Korea: Emerging but Unpredictable Threats

While Russia and China have established themselves as titans of digital subversion, Iran and North Korea are rapidly emerging as unpredictable threats with growing capabilities in hybrid warfare and cyber sabotage.

Iran has a well-documented history of cyber warfare, particularly against its regional rivals. Its *APT33* and *APT34* units have been responsible for numerous attacks on energy companies, financial institutions, and even U.S. infrastructure. The 2012 attack on Saudi Aramco, which destroyed 30,000 computers, was a clear demonstration of Iran's capacity for digital sabotage. Iran's growing expertise in drone technology and asymmetric warfare further adds to its potential for hybrid attacks, combining cyber operations with more traditional military tactics.

Given its strained relationship with the West and its pursuit of nuclear capabilities, Iran has a clear incentive to enhance its cyber warfare abilities, viewing them as a cost-effective means to counterbalance its conventional military weaknesses. Its use of proxy groups, such as Hezbollah, adds another layer of complexity, as these groups can be used to carry out operations with plausible deniability, making attribution difficult.

North Korea, though economically isolated, has rapidly developed into a formidable cyber actor, primarily through its *Lazarus Group*. Initially focused on financial crimes such as bank heists and cryptocurrency theft to fund its regime, North Korea has increasingly shifted towards more politically motivated cyber operations. As mentioned in Chapter 2, North Korea's pursuit of nuclear weapons also includes research into EMP technology, which could be used to cripple the infrastructure of its enemies, particularly South Korea and the United States.

Like Iran, North Korea views cyber operations as a means of levelling the playing field against technologically superior adversaries. Their approach is often audacious, with high-profile hacks, such as the 2014 attack on Sony Pictures, demonstrating a willingness to target civilian institutions to send political messages. Despite their limited resources, North Korea has proven itself capable of significant damage in the cyber domain, posing a wildcard threat that cannot be underestimated.

Conclusion

The evolution of hybrid warfare in the digital age has introduced new dimensions to the concept of national security. Hostile actors like Russia, China, Iran, and North Korea possess not only the intent but also the technical capabilities to engage in chip and circuit sabotage, potentially devastating national infrastructures and economies. These actors operate across a spectrum of tactics ranging from Russia's sophisticated cyber warfare and EMP capabilities to China's dominance over the global tech supply chain and Iran and North Korea's unpredictable and developing cyber arsenals.

In this world of interconnected systems, reliance on technology has become both a strength and a vulnerability. The actors profiled in this chapter represent the most pressing threats to global stability, with each leveraging unique tools to achieve their geopolitical aims. As future conflicts emerge, the focus on chip and circuit sabotage will only intensify, making it imperative for nations to develop robust countermeasures and safeguard their critical infrastructure against these hostile intents.

This chapter lays the groundwork for understanding how these known bad actors operate within the broader spectrum of hybrid warfare, setting the stage for further exploration of defence mechanisms in the chapters that follow. The stakes are clear: the next great conflict may not begin with a bomb or a missile but with the silent infiltration of a single microchip.

Chapter 9: Resilience in the Age of Sabotage: Protecting Critical Technology

Introduction

In an era where hybrid warfare increasingly targets the infrastructure that supports modern life, resilience has become a fundamental concept. Sabotage, especially against the intricate technologies underpinning everything from national defence to healthcare, poses an existential threat to nations and their civilian populations. The resilience of critical technologies, particularly in the face of electronic sabotage such as EMP attacks or supply chain infiltration, requires a robust strategy that integrates technological, governmental, and private sector efforts. This chapter explores the key areas of resilience: from EMP-hardened circuits and supply chain security measures to resilient network protocols, and how both government initiatives and private sector innovations can bolster the nation's defence against sabotage.

Strategies and Technologies to Harden National Infrastructure

The modern state faces a complex and evolving range of threats to its technological infrastructure, which requires a multifaceted approach. While much attention has been given to traditional military defence, the attack surface has expanded into digital and electronic domains, making the hardening of critical infrastructure a national imperative.

EMP-Hardened Circuits

Electromagnetic pulse (EMP) attacks have gained notoriety as one of the most devastating forms of sabotage in the digital age. EMPs can cripple entire electrical grids by overloading and destroying microchips and circuits (as covered in Chapter 2: "EMP: The Silent Weapon"). Historically, the Starfish Prime nuclear test demonstrated the real-world effects of an EMP, and nations like North Korea, Russia, and China have since been suspected of developing EMP weapons capable of massive disruption. To mitigate this, modern circuits are being designed with EMP hardening as a primary consideration.

EMP-hardened circuits are built to absorb and dissipate the energy from EMPs, preventing the damage typically associated with such attacks. Special materials, like ferrite cores and semiconductors engineered for higher resistance, are critical in protecting the electronics that maintain national infrastructure, including power grids, communication systems, and defence mechanisms.

Supply Chain Security Measures

In addition to EMP attacks, the globalized supply chain itself is a weak point, as explored in Chapter 5: "The Threat of Supply Chain Compromise." The insertion of malicious hardware, "kill switches," or compromised firmware into critical electronics is a serious and ongoing concern. The vulnerability of key sectors like defence, healthcare, and aerospace to such sabotage requires the institution of rigorous supply chain security measures.

This includes the verification and authentication of components through blockchain-based tracking systems, forensic auditing of suppliers, and enhancing transparency between manufacturers and end-users. Countries have begun to mandate stronger oversight, with the U.S. Department of Defence and the European Union implementing measures to secure the defence technology supply chains against both physical and digital tampering.

Resilient Network Protocols

Resilience at the network level is equally critical. The reliance on digital communication networks for everything from national security to civilian life (detailed in Chapter 7: "A Nation at Risk") makes them prime targets for attacks, whether through malware, ransomware, or direct network sabotage. To counter this, resilient network protocols have been developed.

Protocols designed with redundancy in mind ensure that when parts of a network are compromised, communication can continue through alternative pathways. Mesh networking, for example, creates multiple routes for data to travel, preventing any single point of failure. Quantum encryption is also gaining traction as a method of securing communications, offering a future-proof solution to eavesdropping or hacking attempts. Governments and corporations alike are investing heavily in such technologies to ensure their networks remain operational during attacks.

Government Initiatives

Governments worldwide have recognized the growing threats posed by cyber warfare, EMPs, and supply chain sabotage. In the U.S., several initiatives have been launched to address these challenges, with agencies and commissions dedicated to ensuring the resilience of critical infrastructure.

EMP Commission

In response to the increasing threat of EMPs, the U.S. Congress established the Electromagnetic Pulse Commission (EMP Commission) to assess the nation's vulnerability and develop strategies for mitigation. The commission's findings highlighted the fragility of America's power grids and the far-reaching consequences of an EMP strike, prompting a range of protective measures, including the implementation of EMP-hardened infrastructure in key areas. The EMP Commission has worked closely with both private industry and the military to implement these solutions, recognizing that a coordinated response is required across all sectors of the economy.

Cybersecurity Directives

Alongside EMP defences, cybersecurity has been a top priority. The U.S. National Cybersecurity Strategy, underpinned by directives such as the Cybersecurity Information Sharing Act (CISA), seeks to create an environment of shared intelligence between government entities and the private sector. These initiatives aim to anticipate and counteract cyber threats before they can inflict damage on critical systems. By developing frameworks for real-time threat sharing and response coordination, these initiatives enhance the resilience of national infrastructure.

Private Sector Role

While the government plays a crucial role in setting policies and providing defence frameworks, the private sector bears significant responsibility for the security and resilience of both consumer and industrial electronics. As discussed in previous chapters, much of the global supply chain, particularly for semiconductors and microchips, is in private hands. Therefore, innovations in these industries are key to safeguarding national infrastructure.

Corporate Responsibility in Security

Corporations are increasingly being held accountable for ensuring that the products they bring to market are free from vulnerabilities, both at the hardware and software levels. In the wake of incidents like the SolarWinds breach (examined in Chapter 4: "Malicious Code"), there has been growing pressure on companies to conduct rigorous security testing of their products before they reach consumers. This extends to industries as diverse as telecommunications, automotive, and medical technology, all of which rely on secure microchips and embedded systems.

In addition, technology companies are leading efforts to design systems that are intrinsically resilient to sabotage. For instance, the incorporation of self-healing networks and fail-safe protocols can minimize the impact of an attack by automatically rerouting data and operations to secure systems.

Innovations to Enhance Security

The private sector has been instrumental in developing cutting-edge technologies to enhance resilience against sabotage. Some key innovations include:

- **Artificial Intelligence (AI) in Threat Detection**: AI algorithms can monitor and analyze massive datasets in real time, detecting anomalies and potential sabotage attempts faster than human operators. AI-powered systems are already in place in many sectors, identifying patterns that may signal an impending cyberattack or hardware failure.

- **Blockchain for Supply Chain Integrity**: Blockchain technology is transforming the way critical components are tracked throughout the supply chain. By providing an immutable ledger of where and when each component is produced and handled, blockchain can help prevent the introduction of malicious hardware or software into national infrastructure systems.

- **Quantum-Resistant Encryption**: With the eventual rise of quantum computing, traditional encryption methods will become obsolete. The private sector is at the forefront of developing quantum-resistant algorithms that can protect data even in the face of quantum-level threats.

Conclusion

Resilience in the age of sabotage is not just a technological challenge it is a national imperative. From EMP-hardened circuits and secure supply chains to resilient network protocols, nations must embrace an integrated approach to safeguarding their critical infrastructures. This requires not only robust government initiatives like the EMP Commission and cybersecurity directives but also proactive engagement from the private sector, which plays a critical role in both developing and deploying the technologies that underpin national resilience.

In a world where hybrid warfare targets the most fundamental aspects of modern life, the ability to protect critical technology from sabotage will define the security and prosperity of nations in the 21st century. The lessons learned from previous attacks, detailed throughout this book, must inform the strategies that nations employ to ensure their infrastructure remains secure, resilient, and ready to face the ever-evolving threats of tomorrow.

Chapter 10: The Role of Cyber Espionage in Hybrid Warfare

Overview: Cyber Espionage as a Force Multiplier in Hybrid Warfare

Hybrid warfare represents the fusion of traditional military tactics with unconventional strategies, such as cyber-attacks, disinformation, economic pressure, and irregular combat. Central to this form of conflict is cyber espionage, which has evolved into one of the most critical tools in the modern arsenal. Espionage in the cyber domain facilitates hybrid warfare through the theft of critical technologies, and plans, and the insertion of vulnerabilities into an adversary's infrastructure, setting the stage for future attacks. This chapter delves into how cyber espionage operates as a silent but deadly precursor to more overt aggression, using sophisticated methods to weaken nations before the conflict even begins.

Espionage is no longer limited to covert operatives physically infiltrating government buildings or military bases. The rise of global connectivity has enabled a new form of espionage where hostile actors remotely access and compromise systems of strategic value. The targets of these operations include everything from sensitive government data and military secrets to industrial designs and emerging technologies, especially those critical to national defence and economic prosperity. This theft is more than an act of covert intelligence gathering; it destabilizes a nation's technological and military edge, undermining its ability to defend itself in the face of overt attacks.

Moreover, the insertion of digital vulnerabilities whether in the form of malware, backdoors, or logic bombs into critical systems during peacetime facilitates easy access during wartime. By strategically placing cyber traps and malicious code, an adversary can cripple or control critical systems during a conflict, whether that be by disabling power grids, disrupting communications, or even interfering with the command and control networks of military forces.

Known Actors: Key Players in Cyber Espionage

The global landscape of cyber espionage is dominated by a few key actors, with China and Russia leading the charge. Their cyber espionage units are often extensions of state military and intelligence apparatuses, capable of conducting sophisticated long-term operations.

China: Among the most well-documented cyber espionage actors is China, particularly in its exploitation of global technological supply chains. China's espionage apparatus is deeply embedded in both its military (People's Liberation Army) and civilian sectors. Groups such as Advanced Persistent Threat 10 (APT10), widely known for their "Cloud Hopper" campaign, have systematically targeted global technology companies, gaining access to proprietary information, software designs, and intellectual property. This not only grants China a competitive edge in various sectors but also positions it to exploit vulnerabilities in these technologies during a conflict.

China's cyber espionage capabilities are particularly concerning due to its potential plans to invade Taiwan, a global leader in the semiconductor industry. Taiwan's semiconductor manufacturing is crucial to global electronics, from smartphones to advanced military hardware. If China were to seize control of Taiwan's chip industry, it would have an enormous advantage in both military and economic domains, gaining access to cutting-edge technologies that power the modern world. As part of a hybrid warfare strategy, China could use cyber espionage to compromise Taiwanese chip manufacturers, such as TSMC, not only to weaken Taiwan's defences but also to monopolize the global semiconductor supply chain.

Russia: Russia's cyber capabilities, particularly through military hacking units such as Fancy Bear (APT28) and the GRU, have been demonstrated in numerous cyberattacks on critical infrastructure worldwide. Russian cyber espionage efforts focus on both military and civilian targets, aiming to gather intelligence, sabotage operations, and destabilize political systems. Russia has been implicated in a series of high-profile cyber campaigns, including the infamous attacks on the U.S. Democratic National Committee in 2016 and its continuous cyber activities aimed at NATO allies.

Russia has also pioneered the integration of cyber espionage with physical warfare, as seen in its hybrid operations during the Ukraine conflict. By blending cyber intrusions with kinetic military actions, Russia has set the blueprint for future hybrid warfare campaigns. For instance, in the 2015 and 2016 cyberattacks on Ukraine's power grid, Russia demonstrated how cyber sabotage can disrupt a nation's critical infrastructure while traditional forces advance on the ground.

The Invasion of Taiwan and Its Semiconductor Industry

China's potential invasion of Taiwan looms as a significant flashpoint in global geopolitics. Taiwan's semiconductor industry is not just an economic powerhouse; it is a strategic asset upon which the global tech sector relies. If China were to seize control of Taiwan, the implications would reverberate across both the civilian and military domains worldwide. Semiconductors are the backbone of modern technology, found in everything from consumer electronics to advanced weapon systems.

Before any military invasion, China is likely to leverage its cyber espionage capabilities to weaken Taiwan's defences. Through sustained cyber campaigns, China could infiltrate Taiwanese semiconductor companies, implanting malicious software or backdoors in their manufacturing processes. These vulnerabilities would give China the ability to compromise the global supply chain, manipulate the market, or even control the production of advanced chips used in Western defence technologies.

Moreover, the global reliance on Taiwanese semiconductors creates a significant strategic vulnerability for nations such as the United States, which is heavily dependent on Taiwan for the chips used in its most advanced military systems. A successful Chinese invasion of Taiwan, facilitated by pre-emptive cyber espionage, would not only alter the balance of power in East Asia but also critically undermine the technological superiority of the West.

Case Study: Operation Cloud Hopper (APT10)

Operation Cloud Hopper, attributed to the Chinese hacking group APT10, exemplifies the broad scope and devastating potential of cyber espionage in hybrid warfare. This sophisticated, long-term campaign targeted global technology service providers, allowing Chinese intelligence to gain access to the networks of multiple corporations worldwide. Through the exploitation of managed service providers (MSPs), APT10 infiltrated the systems of various industries, including healthcare, telecommunications, and aerospace, extracting sensitive data and intellectual property.

By compromising MSPs, APT10 effectively breached the digital defences of their clients, inserting vulnerabilities that could be used for future sabotage or espionage operations. This operation underscores the broader strategy of cyber espionage: to gather intelligence and exploit technological weaknesses long before any physical conflict. The information stolen during Cloud Hopper could potentially be weaponized in future conflicts, granting China the ability to sabotage or undermine critical sectors in adversary nations.

Furthermore, this case highlights the vulnerability of interconnected global industries to cyber intrusions. As companies outsource their IT services to third-party providers, the risk of wide-reaching cyber espionage increases exponentially. APT10's success in Operation Cloud Hopper serves as a wake-up call for the importance of securing the entire digital supply chain, from service providers to end-users.

Conclusion: The Unseen Threat of Cyber Espionage

Cyber espionage has transformed the nature of modern conflict, allowing states to engage in warfare without firing a single shot. By infiltrating critical networks, stealing valuable information, and planting digital traps, cyber espionage provides the groundwork for future physical confrontations, while destabilizing adversaries long before any visible action is taken. In the context of hybrid warfare, the role of cyber espionage is clear: it serves as both the silent assassin and the advance scout, weakening a nation from within and leaving it vulnerable to further exploitation or invasion.

As global tensions rise, particularly in regions like East Asia, cyber espionage will continue to play a central role in the strategies of dominant powers like China and Russia. Understanding and countering these covert operations is critical to maintaining national security in the digital age.

In the following chapter, we will explore how the world's major powers can build resilience against these types of attacks and protect their critical infrastructure in the face of an increasingly hostile cyber landscape.

Chapter 11: Global Deterrence and the Geopolitical Fallout

Overview: The Age of Technological Sabotage

In an increasingly interconnected world, the battlefield is no longer confined to land, sea, or air; it extends into the digital realm. Modern warfare now encompasses a sophisticated array of tools, with technological sabotage emerging as one of the most disruptive. This form of warfare, often executed through cyberattacks, compromises to critical infrastructure, and sabotage of technological systems, poses a grave threat to national security and international stability.

Technological sabotage be it through cyberattacks on power grids, hacking into sensitive defence networks, or the insertion of malicious code in supply chains has profound global implications. In Chapter 6, we explored how attacks on critical infrastructure can cripple national systems, and in Chapter 4, the insidious nature of malicious code was discussed. Now, we turn to how this form of sabotage is increasingly used by state and non-state actors as a strategic tool in modern warfare. The question at hand is not merely whether such acts will continue, but how the world can deter them and respond to the fallout that follows when deterrence fails.

Potential for Escalation: From Sabotage to War

The line between sabotage and military conflict is a tenuous one, and technological sabotage has the potential to push global powers toward broader military engagements. As outlined in previous chapters, attacks on national infrastructure can paralyze critical services, disrupt economies, and severely degrade a nation's ability to defend itself. For instance, the cascading effects of a blackout or disruption of supply chains (as discussed in Chapter 5) can trigger economic crises, and social unrest, and leave military forces exposed to further attacks.

Infrastructure as a Catalyst for War

The escalation risk is particularly high when national infrastructure is targeted. Power grids, transportation networks, and communication systems often controlled by highly vulnerable Supervisory Control and Data Acquisition (SCADA) systems (Chapter 6) are vital for the operation of any modern state. An attack on such infrastructure could be perceived as an act of war, prompting military retaliation. As we saw in the case of Russia's cyberattacks on Ukraine's power grid, these incidents are often precursors to broader geopolitical moves (Chapter 6).

However, the risk of escalation is not limited to traditional warfare. The digital domain is inherently connected to the physical one, and technological sabotage in cyberspace can cause real-world damage. A state experiencing crippling cyberattacks may feel justified in responding with kinetic force. In such a scenario, an initial cyberattack could serve as the trigger for a much larger and more destructive military conflict.

Cyberattacks on Critical Infrastructure as a Precursor to Invasion

Consider the possibility of an attack on Taiwan's semiconductor industry, a critical global supplier of microchips, which was analyzed in Chapter 10. Such an attack would not only cripple Taiwan but would also have massive repercussions for the global economy. The U.S., European Union, and other global powers that rely on Taiwanese chips for everything from consumer electronics to defence systems could find themselves dragged into a wider conflict. This exemplifies how an act of technological sabotage particularly in a highly interconnected global economy could have far-reaching, even catastrophic, consequences.

Known Responses: Strengthening defences and Offensive Cyber Capabilities

Recognizing the growing threat of technological sabotage, global powers have responded by enhancing their cybersecurity frameworks, developing offensive cyber capabilities, and engaging in diplomatic initiatives aimed at deterrence.

NATO's Cyber defence Initiatives

NATO has significantly ramped up its cyber defence posture in response to the growing number of cyberattacks targeting its member states. The establishment of the NATO Cooperative Cyber Defence Centre of Excellence (CCDCOE) in Tallinn, Estonia, and the development of a formalized cyber defence policy demonstrates the alliance's commitment to confronting this modern threat. Chapter 9's discussion on resilience strategies highlighted the importance of national initiatives; NATO, as a collective security organization, amplifies this by ensuring that cyberattacks on one member state are treated as a collective concern. This is essential in a world where an attack on critical infrastructure, such as energy grids or communication systems, could have cascading effects across borders.

NATO's cyber policy not only aims to defend its members but also serves as a deterrent. Article 5, the cornerstone of NATO's defence policy, traditionally focused on kinetic military attacks, has been extended to include large-scale cyberattacks. The threat of collective retaliation for a cyberattack provides a degree of deterrence, but the rapid evolution of cyber weapons means that NATO must continuously adapt its defences.

U.S. Cyber Command's Offensive Capabilities

While defensive measures are critical, deterrence often requires the credible threat of retaliation. The United States has been at the forefront of developing offensive cyber capabilities through the U.S. Cyber Command. Chapter 10 touched on the U.S. government's capabilities in cyber espionage and hybrid warfare, but U.S. Cyber Command goes beyond surveillance. Its ability to launch pre-emptive or retaliatory cyberattacks against adversaries sends a strong message to potential aggressors: any act of technological sabotage against U.S. interests will be met with significant consequences.

For example, in 2018, U.S. Cyber Command conducted offensive operations against Russian cyber actors attempting to interfere in the midterm elections. This operation demonstrated that offensive cyber measures are not limited to wartime scenarios but can also be deployed to protect democratic processes. By taking a more aggressive stance, the U.S. hopes to deter not just nation-states, but also non-state actors, from engaging in cyber sabotage.

The Limits of Deterrence and the Risk of Miscalculation

However, deterrence in the cyber domain is fraught with challenges. Cyberattacks can be difficult to attribute with certainty, making retaliation a politically complex decision. Moreover, as Chapter 8 outlined, the range of bad actors with the technical capability to engage in cyber sabotage is growing. Russia, China, Iran, and North Korea all possess significant cyber warfare capabilities. The challenge for global powers is to distinguish between acts of state-sponsored sabotage and those conducted by independent hacking groups.

The risk of miscalculation also looms large. An act of cyber sabotage might be interpreted as the first step in a larger campaign of hybrid warfare (Chapter 1), prompting a state to escalate before fully understanding the nature or source of the attack. The risk of unintentional escalation is compounded by the fact that cyberattacks, once initiated, are difficult to contain. Malicious code introduced into one system can spread uncontrollably, impacting unintended targets and potentially drawing multiple nations into a conflict.

The Geopolitical Fallout: A Fractured Global Order

Technological sabotage has the potential to reshape the global geopolitical landscape. As states become more reliant on digital infrastructure, those that can effectively sabotage these systems gain a significant strategic advantage. The weaponization of cyberspace and technological sabotage will likely exacerbate existing tensions between major powers, and new geopolitical fault lines are emerging.

The U.S.-China Cyber Rivalry

The ongoing U.S.-China cyber rivalry is a case in point. As explored in Chapter 10, Chinese cyber espionage groups have been linked to large-scale theft of intellectual property, particularly in the tech and defence sectors. China's dominance in the global chip supply chain gives it both a strategic advantage and a vulnerability. In the event of a full-scale conflict, particularly over Taiwan, China's cyber capabilities would likely play a central role in its strategy, potentially disrupting the global chip industry and severely affecting Western economies.

The Erosion of Trust and Global Cooperation

The global fallout from cyber sabotage extends beyond the immediate effects of an attack. As states grow increasingly suspicious of one another's cyber intentions, trust between nations erodes. This is particularly dangerous in the context of international cooperation on issues like climate change, public health, and economic development, where global cooperation is essential.

In the private sector, technological sabotage particularly when targeting supply chains could lead to the re-shoring of industries, as states seek to reduce their reliance on foreign-made components (Chapter 5). This could further fragment the global economy, leading to increased protectionism and economic instability.

Conclusion: Navigating the Future of Global Deterrence

The age of technological sabotage is here, and its implications are vast. While NATO, the U.S. Cyber Command, and other global actors are developing frameworks for deterrence and response, the risk of miscalculation and escalation remains high. Cyberattacks on critical infrastructure could trigger broader conflicts, while the geopolitical fallout from such attacks threatens to fracture the global order. The challenge for the future lies in building resilient systems (Chapter 9) and developing international norms that govern the use of cyber weapons, ensuring that the digital age does not lead to perpetual conflict.

Chapter 12: The Future of Warfare: An Arms Race in the Digital Domain

Overview

As we move deeper into the 21st century, the nature of warfare is undergoing a profound transformation. Traditional battlefields, characterized by tanks, soldiers, and missiles, are being eclipsed by an arena that is both invisible and omnipresent: cyberspace. In this new theatre of war, the weapons are no longer steel and lead, but chips and code. Data, once seen primarily as an asset, has become a weapon, and the battlefield is increasingly the digital realm where information is manipulated, systems are sabotaged, and entire nations can be destabilized with a few keystrokes.

This evolution is not just a change in tactics but represents a shift in the very paradigm of conflict. In previous chapters, we examined the critical vulnerability of infrastructure, the susceptibility of supply chains, and the increasing reliance on cyber espionage. Now, these threats converge in an even more formidable form: a global arms race focused not on nuclear stockpiles, but on digital superiority. At the heart of this new race are artificial intelligence (AI), machine learning, and autonomous systems, which are already reshaping the military landscape.

The next wars may be fought without a single soldier setting foot on enemy soil. Instead, they will be conducted through attacks on embedded systems, the manipulation of critical infrastructure, and sophisticated AI-driven assaults designed to cripple economies, military capabilities, and social stability without the need for confrontation.

Predictions: AI-Driven Attacks and Autonomous Cyber Sabotage

As artificial intelligence becomes increasingly integrated into both civilian and military sectors, the risk of AI-driven attacks on embedded systems grows. These systems, which are integral to everything from national defence to economic operations, present high-value targets for adversaries seeking to cripple a nation without firing a shot. Unlike conventional attacks, which often rely on brute force or human ingenuity, AI-driven cyber sabotage leverages machine learning algorithms that evolve with each engagement, adapting to defences and exploiting weaknesses at unprecedented speeds.

AI's capacity for rapid data processing and decision-making could lead to the development of autonomous cyber weapons systems capable of identifying vulnerabilities, launching attacks, and self-replicating across networks without human intervention. Such weapons could target critical infrastructure, military command and control systems, or financial institutions, causing cascading failures that would paralyze nations and their economies.

A key concern in this scenario is that AI-driven warfare operates at a scale and speed that could outpace human decision-making. If left unchecked, autonomous systems could initiate conflict without human oversight, leading to accidental escalations that spiral out of control. The real threat lies in their potential to be used for preemptive strikes, where the line between offensive and defensive actions becomes blurred.

Leadership: The Need for Strong Governance in the Western World

At the heart of countering these emerging threats is the need for strong, decisive leadership, particularly within the United States, Canada, the United Kingdom, and Western Europe. In this high-stakes environment, the role of leadership is to recognize that warfare has fundamentally shifted and to adopt policies and strategies that reflect this reality. Weak or indecisive governance risks leaving nations vulnerable to digital sabotage, much as appeasement policies in the early 20th century emboldened aggressive powers to push the boundaries of acceptable conflict.

Leftist and globalist political movements, which often prioritize diplomatic appeasement over strong defensive postures, may inadvertently open the door to conflict by failing to recognize the necessity of hard power in the digital domain. While diplomacy and cooperation remain vital, they must be balanced with the recognition that nations like China and Russia are actively pursuing dominance in cyber warfare and that the digital battlefield is as real and consequential as any physical one.

The West's survival in this new era hinges on its ability to foster technological innovation, secure its digital infrastructure, and adopt a posture of strength in cyber defence and offence. Only through strong, forward-thinking leadership can Western nations hope to deter aggression in the digital domain and maintain their sovereignty.

The Role of International Cooperation

The global nature of cyberspace requires a coordinated international response to the threats posed by cyber warfare. While nations must bolster their defences, the interconnectedness of global networks means that an attack on one country can quickly have cascading effects on others. International cooperation, particularly among Western allies, will be key to creating a robust and resilient defence against digital threats.

However, cooperation alone is insufficient. It must be coupled with deterrence. As outlined in **Chapter 11: Global Deterrence and the Geopolitical Fallout**, the ability to respond to cyberattacks with equal or greater force is a critical element of modern military strategy. Deterrence in the digital domain may involve both overt and covert capabilities, ranging from the public display of advanced cyber defence systems to the quiet development of offensive tools capable of retaliating against attacks in real time.

Balancing diplomacy with deterrence will require a delicate approach. Diplomatic channels must remain open to prevent unnecessary escalations, but they cannot come at the expense of security. As seen with NATO's cyber defence initiatives and the U.S. Cyber Command's development of offensive cyber capabilities, alliances play a crucial role in maintaining a balance of power in this new digital arms race.

Furthermore, **economic strength** plays a pivotal role in funding the kind of technological advancements needed to defend against and deter cyber threats. In a world where technology is the battlefield, nations with stronger economies will be better positioned to lead the digital arms race. Investing in research, development, and cybersecurity infrastructure is not just a matter of national security it is a prerequisite for survival in the digital age.

Conclusion

As the future of warfare moves increasingly into the digital realm, it is clear that the nature of conflict is changing in fundamental ways. The battlefield is now cyberspace, and the weapons of war are no longer guns and bombs, but algorithms and chips. The rise of AI-driven attacks and autonomous cyber sabotage marks a new era in military conflict, one in which speed, adaptability, and innovation will be the deciding factors.

Leadership within Western nations must recognize the gravity of this shift. The policies of appeasement and inaction that have characterized certain political movements are ill-suited to the realities of digital warfare. Strong, decisive leadership is required to secure national interests, safeguard infrastructure, and prevent adversaries from gaining an advantage in this new theatre of war.

Finally, international cooperation will be essential in managing the risks posed by cyber warfare. Deterrence must be balanced with diplomacy, and economic strength will underpin the West's ability to innovate and defend against increasingly sophisticated digital threats. In the end, the future of warfare may be fought on the invisible front lines of cyberspace, but its consequences will be as real and devastating as any conflict humanity has ever known.

Epilogue: A World at the Brink

As we stand at the dawn of a new era in warfare, it is no longer soldiers, tanks, and missiles that define global conflict. Instead, our world's power dynamics are increasingly shaped by the chips embedded in our infrastructure and the code running beneath our digital systems. The invisible war of sabotage, espionage, and cyber assaults has ushered in an age where the battlefield is no longer a distant land, but the circuits and signals that power modern civilization.

The preceding chapters have illuminated how advanced technological warfare through cyber sabotage, EMP strikes, and supply chain compromise poses an existential threat to every nation's security. From the subtle espionage of compromised hardware to the devastating consequences of large-scale infrastructure collapse, the implications are vast and dire. The case studies and examples demonstrate the alarming proficiency of state and non-state actors in exploiting digital weaknesses, and the stakes for not addressing these vulnerabilities could not be higher.

At the heart of this conflict lies the fragile nature of the interconnected systems we have come to rely on. The very innovations that have propelled humanity into a technological golden age have also become its Achilles' heel. Embedded systems, communications networks, and global supply chains are deeply vulnerable to exploitation by hostile actors, whose primary aim is not to conquer territories but to cripple economies, devastate societies, and diminish the power of their rivals.

Yet the future remains unwritten. While the threats posed by hybrid warfare, digital sabotage, and EMPs are formidable, they are not insurmountable. The chapters in this book illustrate a central theme: the solution to these unprecedented challenges lies in resilience, cooperation, and leadership.

Nations must move beyond traditional geopolitical strategies and engage in a modern arms race of cyber defence and offensive capabilities. As was evident in the discussions on global deterrence, the failure to adapt to the rapid pace of technological change leaves countries exposed not only to disruption but to devastation. In the face of sabotage, collaboration between international allies particularly between the U.S., Canada, the UK, and Western Europe is critical. Leadership in these regions must prioritize fortifying cyber defences while balancing diplomacy with the necessary resolve to deter bad actors from escalating tensions into full-scale warfare.

But this effort cannot be borne by governments alone. The private sector, from tech giants to manufacturers, must play a pivotal role. Companies must recognize that in today's interconnected world, they are as much targets as they are protectors. Innovations in cyber security, EMP-hardened systems, and the management of secure supply chains will be essential to prevent the kinds of attacks that can cripple industries and economies overnight.

The key lesson from this book is that the future of conflict, while shaped by technology, is ultimately a human endeavour. It requires foresight, resilience, and a willingness to act before it's too late. Strong leadership and decisive action are required not only to defend the systems we depend on but also to ensure that those who seek to exploit them are met with unified, unyielding resistance.

The arms race of the 21st century is not fought with steel but with silicon. Nations must ensure their survival by preparing for a future in which sabotage can come not from the sky or the sea, but from the digital depths of cyberspace. The stakes are no less than the preservation of the technological foundation upon which modern life depends.

If we fail to act, the chips may indeed be fried and with them, the very fabric of our civilization.

John Shenton

End

Don't miss out!

Visit the website below and you can sign up to receive emails whenever John Shenton publishes a new book. There's no charge and no obligation.

https://books2read.com/r/B-A-RJUO-LWSAF

BOOKS 2 READ

Connecting independent readers to independent writers.

Did you love *Fried Chips*? Then you should read *The Dragon's Gambit: China's Bid for Global Dominance and the Western Response*[1] by John Shenton!

In the 21st century, few challenges loom as large on the global stage as the rapid rise of China, and it's bid to assert dominance in every sphere of international influence. The Dragon's Gambit: China's Bid for Global Dominance and the Western Response provides a detailed, multifaceted exploration of this phenomenon, offering readers a critical examination of China's strategic ambitions and the global repercussions. This book does more than recount history—it dissects China's current manoeuvres, scrutinizing the far-reaching consequences and posing urgent questions for the West's response.

---

1. https://books2read.com/u/bzyZ9E

2. https://books2read.com/u/bzyZ9E

Also by John Shenton

Business Plan Basics
The Bahamas - More Islands and Recipes Than You Expect!
Collected Musings from Bricks and Mortar to E-commerce
The Smart City Odyssey: Unveiling the Secrets to Traveller-Centric
Software
The Dragon's Gambit: China's Bid for Global Dominance and the
Western Response
Silent Weapon
Business Basics: Money Sources
Influx
Fried Chips
Mandates, Motors, and Misinformation
Echos of Orwell
Control and Chaos
The Empire's Warning: What Rome's Fall Tells Us About the West
Today

About the Author

John Shenton was born in Birmingham, England and grew up in postwar England. He spent several years as a Radio Officer onboard a variety of vessels sailing to the Persian Gulf, the Indian Ocean and South China seas.

With degrees and a background in electronics and computers he has lived and worked within the United Kingdom, Germany, Switzerland and Canada.

While doing so, he established numerous trading relationships in Japan, Korea, the USA, China and other countries.

He has been retired for some time now living in Montréal Canada enjoying golfing, writing, sailing and many other things automotive.

About the Publisher

John Shenton published via Draft2digital